This Trip Tracker is the property of...

Name: _____

Address: _____

_____

_____

Phone
Number: _____

Birthday: _____

Here's what I look like.

(Draw a picture or paste a photo here.)

I'm on my way to _____.

I'm traveling by _____

Trip Calendar

Here's my itinerary—where I'm going and when.

Month _____

Sun.	Mon.	Tues.	Wed.	Thurs.	Fri.	Sat.

As far as predictions go, I'm most looking

forward to _____.

I can't wait to see how things turn out!

Cast of Characters

Here's the inside story on my travel companions.

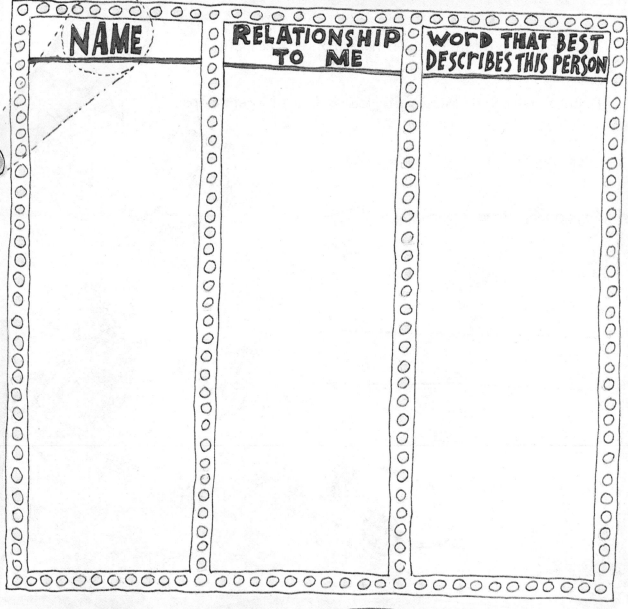

NAME	RELATIONSHIP TO ME	WORD THAT BEST DESCRIBES THIS PERSON

I'm sure I'll have more to say about them later.

Getting Ready

Things to do before I leave:

- [ ] Read about places I'm going to visit.

- [ ] Check out these places on a map.

- [ ] Write to city and state tourist offices. (Lots of free stuff!)

- [ ] Fill out names and addresses in my journal. (Don't forget stamps!)

- [ ] Pack. (Maybe Mom or Dad will help me.)

- [ ] Say goodbye to my friends.

- [ ] Get really excited!

- [ ] _____

- [ ] _____

- [ ] _____

Packing Checklist

This is what I plan to bring on my trip.

Stuff to BRING

PACKED

_____   _____

_____   _____

_____   _____

_____   _____

_____   _____

_____   _____

_____   _____

_____   _____

The most important thing to remember to pack is my _____.

I never travel without it!

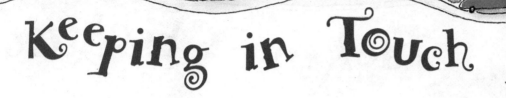

Keeping in Touch

These are some of the people I might write to on my trip.

- [ ] The President
- [ ] Best friend
- [ ] Neighbor
- [ ] Doctor
- [ ] Whoever wrote me last
- [ ] ~~Girlfriend or Boyfriend~~ FORGET IT!
- [ ] Pet
- [ ] Favorite stuffed animal

- [ ] Pizza delivery kid
- [ ] Teacher
- [ ] Parents
- [ ] Grandparents
- [ ] Aunts and Uncles
- [ ] Cousins
- [ ] Teammates
- [ ] Other_____

Date →

greeting →

April 1, 2010
Dear Ima,
I'm having the most
awesome, fantastic, coolest
time ever! I hope your
vacation has been just as great.

message →

I'll see you soon,

closing →

Best regards,

your name →

Yuri Pal

Ima Friend
2 Yew St.
Anytown, Anyplace 12345

Don't forget
a stamp.
(Stamp out
forgetfulness!)

name +
address of
person
you're
writing
to

Get busy writing!
Did you think you were
on vacation or something?

Names and Addresses

I've put the names and addresses of old
and new friends here so I can write to them.

Name:
"Spot"

Names + Addresses

Names + Addresses

Address:
1 Shady Tree Lane
Backyardsville, MI K9K9K

Spot

Passport

I've checked off all the places I've been on this trip—and even some I've visited before.

Alabama (AL)	**Connecticut (CT)**	**Illinois (IL)**	**Maryland (MD)**
Yellowhammer State	Constitution State	Prairie State	Old Line State
Alaska (AK)	**Delaware (DE)**	**Indiana (IN)**	**Massachusetts (MA)**
Last Frontier	Diamond State	Hoosier State	Bay State
Arizona (AZ)	**Florida (FL)**	**Iowa (IA)**	**Michigan (MI)**
Grand Canyon State	Sunshine State	Hawkeye State	Great Lakes State
Arkansas (AR)	**Georgia (GA)**	**Kansas (KS)**	**Minnesota (MN)**
Natural State	Peach State	Sunflower State	North Star State
California (CA)	**Hawaii (HI)**	**Kentucky (KY)**	**Mississippi (MS)**
Golden State	Aloha State	Bluegrass State	Magnolia State
Colorado (CO)	**Idaho (ID)**	**Louisiana (LA)**	**Missouri (MO)**
Centennial State	Gem State	Pelican State	Show Me State
		Maine (ME)	**Montana (MT)**
		Pine Tree State	Big Sky Country

Nebraska (NE)

Cornhusker State

North Dakota (ND)

Peace Garden State

South Dakota (SD)

Coyote State

West Virginia (WV)

Mountain State

Nevada (NV)

Silver State

Ohio (OH)

Buckeye State

Tennessee (TN)

Volunteer State

Wisconsin (WI)

Badger State

New Hampshire (NH)

Granite State

Oklahoma (OK)

Sooner State

Texas (TX)

Lone Star State

Wyoming (WY)

Cowboy State

New Jersey (NJ)

Garden State

Oregon (OR)

Beaver State

Utah (UT)

Beehive State

Washington, D.C.

New Mexico (NM)

Land of Enchantment

Pennsylvania (PA)

Keystone State

Vermont (VT)

Green Mountain State

Canada

New York (NY)

Empire State

Rhode Island (RI)

Ocean State

Virginia (VA)

Old Dominion

Mexico

North Carolina (NC)

Tar Heel State

South Carolina (SC)

Palmetto State

Washington (WA)

Evergreen State

Other

Travel Journal

Today is _____

I am in _____

Best thing I did today _____

Worst thing I did today _____

Other Stuff

FUN·O·METER
Today is...

FUN
↑
NOT
↓

words fail!
totally AWESOME
Cool
pretty FUN
OK
zero fun
BIG PAIN

MOOD CheCk
Today I feel...

- ☐ Cheerful
- ☐ Helpful
- ☐ Homesick
- ☐ Dopey
- ☐ Grumpy
- ☐ Sleepy
- ☐ Bashful
- ☐ Silly
- ☐ Bored
- ☐ Other

2B continued

Weather or Not
Today's weather is...

click click

Travel tips

Here are some tips for an awesome trip.

Stake out your territory.

Show off your map-reading skills.

Here are some more...

Stay energized!

Travel Journal

Today is _____   I am in _____

Here's what made me mad
_____
_____

But this made me laugh
_____
_____

O ther Stuff

2B continued

FUN-O-METER
Today is ...

FUN

NOT

words fail!
totally AWESOME
Cool
Pretty FUN
O.K.
zero fun
BIG PAIN

MOOD Check
Today I feel...

☐ Happy
☐ Lucky
☐ Happy-go-lucky
☐ Perky
☐ Pouty
☐ Stubborn
☐ Playful
☐ Naughty
☐ Nice
☐ Other

Weather or Not
Today's weather is...

Mapping the way

This is a map of my vacation.

Travel Journal

Today is _____ I am in _____

Best travel companion _____

Worst travel companion _____

Other Stuff

FUN·O·METER
today is ...

FUN
NOT

words fail!
totally AWESOME
Cool
Pretty FUN
OK
zero fun
BIG PAIN

MOOD Check

Today I feel...
☐ Funny
☐ Funky
☐ Furious
☐ Angry
☐ Awesome
☐ Anxious
☐ Elated
☐ Eager
☐ Energetic
☐ Other

2B continued

Weather or Not

Today's weather is ...

Autographs

Here's a list of autographs–including family and friends and anyone else I've met along the way.

Travel Journal

Today is _____ I am in _____

_____

Some new foods I've tried _____

_____

But I don't recommend this _____

_____

Other Stuff

FUN·O·METER

Today is...

FUN

NOT

word fail

totally AWESOME

cool

pretty FUN

OK

zero fun

BIG PAIN

MOOD check

Today I feel...

☐ Up
☐ Down
☐ All-around
☐ Good
☐ Bad
☐ Interested
☐ Uninterested
☐ Excited
☐ Bored
☐ Other

2B continued

Weather or Not

Today's weather is...

Memories

Saving stuff like ticket stubs, postcards, and pictures will always remind me of my trip. That's why I put them here.

Travel Journal

Today is _____   I am in _____

What I like about this place _____
_____

What I don't like _____
_____

_O_ther _Stuff_

FUN·O·METER
today is ...

FUN ↑
NOT ↓

words fail
totally AWESOME
Cool
pretty FUN
O.K.
zero fun
BIG PAIN

MOOD CHECK
Today I feel...

☐ Thoughtful
☐ Carefree
☐ Careless
☐ Sporty
☐ Jolly
☐ Goofy
☐ Witty
☐ Friendly
☐ Unfriendly
☐ Other

2B continued

Weather or Not
Today's weather is...

Picture Postcard

On one side of the postcard I've drawn a picture from my trip.
The other side tells all about it.

To:

Travel Journal

Today is _____   I am in _____

Best things to do in the a.m. _____

Best things to do in the p.m. _____

Other Stuff

FUN-O-METER

Today is...

FUN ↑
NOT ↓

- words fail!
- totally AWESOME
- Cool
- pretty FUN
- O.K.
- zero fun
- BIG PAIN

MOOD CHECK

Today I feel...

- ☐ Tip-top
- ☐ Tough
- ☐ Terrible
- ☐ Terrific
- ☐ Tired
- ☐ Happy
- ☐ Hopeful
- ☐ Ho-hum
- ☐ Hurried
- ☐ Other

2B continued

Weather or Not

Today's weather is...

Thumbs Up / Thumbs Down

Here's the best-of-my-trip list.

Here's the worst-of-my-trip list.

Places to go

Things to do

People I've Met ✓

Food & Restaurants

Souvenir

official movie star glasses $5

Travel Journal

Today is _____ I am in _____

Can't wait to do this _____

But I'm sick of this _____

Other Stuff

FUN-O-METER
Today is...

FUN
NOT

words fail!
totally AWESOME
Cool
Pretty FUN
O.K.
zero fun
BIG PAIN

MOOD CheCK
Today I feel...

- [ ] Worried
- [ ] Wonderful
- [ ] Wacky
- [ ] Homesick
- [ ] Carsick
- [ ] Great
- [ ] Grateful
- [ ] Grouchy
- [ ] Optimistic
- [ ] Other

2B continued

Weather or Not
Today's weather is...

click click
click

Here's Me!

These pictures show how I looked at the beginning and end of the day.

Travel Journal

Today is _____

I am in _____

I'm glad I packed this _____

I should've left this at home _____

Other Stuff

FUN-O-METER
Today is...

FUN ↑

NOT ↓

- words fail
- totally AWESOME
- Cool
- pretty FUN
- OK
- zero fun
- BIG PAIN

2B continued

MOOD CHECK
Today I feel...

- ☐ Cheerful
- ☐ Helpful
- ☐ Homesick
- ☐ Dopey
- ☐ Grumpy
- ☐ Sleepy
- ☐ Bashful
- ☐ Silly
- ☐ Bored
- ☐ Other

Weather or Not
Today's weather is...

On the Go!

I've checked off all the types of transportation I've tried on my trip and, just for the record, a few I'd like to try someday.

- ☐ bus
- ☐ dog sled
- ☐ skis
- ☐ helicopter
- ☐ submarine
- ☐ go-cart
- ☐ camel
- ☐ in-line skates
- ☐ train
- ☐ llama
- ☐ burro
- ☐ skateboard
- ☐ motorcycle
- ☐ airplane

- ☐ elephant
- ☐ wheelchair
- ☐ time machine
- ☐ unicycle
- ☐ bicycle
- ☐ foot
- ☐ covered wagon
- ☐ hydrofoil
- ☐ car
- ☐ magic carpet
- ☐ hot-air balloon
- ☐ blimp
- ☐ rickshaw
- ☐ boat

Travel Journal

Today is _____

I am in _____

Coolest thing I saw today _____

Dumbest thing I heard _____

Other Stuff

FUN-O-METER

Today is...

FUN ↑
NOT ↓

- words fail!
- totally AWESOME
- Cool
- Pretty FUN
- O.K.
- zero fun
- BIG PAIN

MOOD Check

Today I feel...

- ☐ Happy
- ☐ Lucky
- ☐ Happy-go-lucky
- ☐ Perky
- ☐ Pouty
- ☐ Stubborn
- ☐ Playful
- ☐ Naughty
- ☐ Nice
- ☐ Other

2B continued

Weather or Not

Today's weather is...

Vacation Lingo

Brother, sister, mother, dad—please shut up you drive me MAD!
I've heard these things one too many times on this trip.

Travel Journal

Today is _____

I am in _____

I can't believe I did this _____

But this was so typical of me _____

Other Stuff

FUN·O·METER
Today is...
FUN
NOT

words fail
totally AWESOME
Cool
Pretty FUN
OK
zero fun
BIG PAIN

MOOD CHECK
Today I feel...
- ☐ Funny
- ☐ Funky
- ☐ Furious
- ☐ Angry
- ☐ Awesome
- ☐ Anxious
- ☐ Elated
- ☐ Eager
- ☐ Energetic
- ☐ Other

2B continued

Weather or Not
Today's weather is...

Traveler's Herald

This was a news-making adventure I had.

THE ★ HERALD

Travel Journal

Today is _____

I am in _____

Best souvenirs so far _____

I wasted my money on this _____

Other Stuff

FUN·O·METER
today is...

FUN

NOT

words fail

totally AWESOME

Cool

Pretty FUN

OK

zero fun

BIG PAIN

2B continued

MOOD CheCK

Today I feel...

- ☐ Up
- ☐ Down
- ☐ All-around
- ☐ Good
- ☐ Bad
- ☐ Interested
- ☐ Uninterested
- ☐ Excited
- ☐ Bored
- ☐ Other

Weather or Not

Today's weather is...

Memories

Saving stuff like ticket stubs, postcards, and pictures will always remind me of my trip. That's why I put them here.

Travel Journal

Today is _____

I am in _____

Most awesome landmarks _____

_____

Worst tourist traps _____

_____

O ther Stuff

2B continued

FUN-O-METER
today is...

FUN ↑

NOT ↓

- words fail!
- totally AWESOME
- Cool
- Pretty FUN
- OK
- zero fun
- BIG PAIN

MOOD check

Today I feel...

- ☐ Thoughtful
- ☐ Carefree
- ☐ Careless
- ☐ Sporty
- ☐ Jolly
- ☐ Goofy
- ☐ Witty
- ☐ Friendly
- ☐ Unfriendly
- ☐ Other

Weather or Not

Today's weather is...

Travel log

Here are my "been there, done that" lists—and a few others, too.

I've
Been There

I've
DONE THAT

I'D
LIKE TO GO THERE

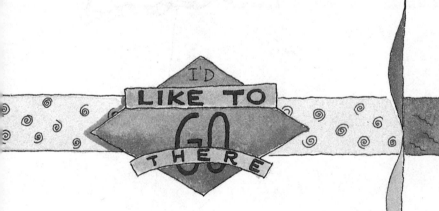

I
NEVER want to go there.

Travel Journal

Today is _____

I am in _____

I always want to remember this _____

But I'd rather forget about this _____

Other Stuff

FUN-O-METER

Today is...

FUN

NOT

words fail

totally AWESOME

Cool

pretty FUN

OK

zero fun

BIG PAIN

MOOD CHECK

Today I feel...

- ☐ Tip-top
- ☐ Tough
- ☐ Terrible
- ☐ Terrific
- ☐ Tired
- ☐ Happy
- ☐ Hopeful
- ☐ Ho-hum
- ☐ Hurried
- ☐ Other

2B continued

Weather or Not

Today's weather is...

click click click

Fantasy Vacation

Here's a picture of the best vacation I can imagine.

Travel Journal

Today is _____

I am in _____

First thing I'll do when I get home _____

But I'm not looking forward to this _____

Other Stuff

FUN·O·METER
Today is...

FUN
NOT

words fail
totally AWESOME
Cool
Pretty FUN
OK
zero fun
BIG PAIN

MOOD Check
Today I feel...
- ☐ Worried
- ☐ Wonderful
- ☐ Wacky
- ☐ Homesick
- ☐ Carsick
- ☐ Great
- ☐ Grateful
- ☐ Grouchy
- ☐ Optimistic
- ☐ Other

2B continued

Weather or Not
Today's weather is...

Wrap-Up

Looking back at my predictions about this trip, I was
- ☐ dreaming.
- ☐ right on target.
- ☐ out of my mind.

In the end, I had
- ☐ way more
- ☐ a little more
- ☐ no more
- ☐ less
- ☐ way less

fun than I thought I would.

sigh.

If anyone offers to take me on a trip again, I'll
- ☐ hide.
- ☐ faint.
- ☐ yawn.
- ☐ pack quickly.
- ☐ jump for joy.

Road-Tested

I Spy

If you are "it," choose an object, like a red button, and say: "I spy with my little eye something red." The other players then take turns trying to guess what the object is. The person who guesses the answer gets to be "it." HINT: Don't give the answer away by staring at the object.

Name That Tune

Players take turns thinking of songs and humming them for one another, a few notes at time, while the others try to be the first to "name that tune." Once you have a tune in mind, hum just the first three notes. If nobody recognizes it, hum the first four notes. Keep adding notes one at a time until someone guesses the name of the song. The first person to guess becomes the next "hummer." (Good whistlers can whistle their tunes.)

Make Me Laugh

This game is serious fun. No kidding! One person becomes the "jester" and the rest are "stonefaces." Stonefaces must never laugh or smile—if they do, their faces break. Of course the jester thinks this is funny and likes nothing more than to make stonefaces crack up. That's the game! The jester has to crack up the stonefaces. The jester can make faces, funny noises, tell jokes, but cannot tickle or touch the stonefaces to make them laugh. The last stoneface to laugh gets to be the next jester.

City Train

If you know the names of a lot of cities, take a ride on the City Train. The rules are simple—players take turns saying the names of cities. The only catch is that each city name must begin with the letter that ended the last one. For example, Houston might be followed by New York, which might be followed by Kansas City, and so on. Any player who can't come up with a city has to get off the train. The last one riding the City Train is the winner. All aboard!

Rochambeau

This game, sometimes called "Rock, Paper, Scissors," works best with two or three players. These are the rules—paper (flat hand) covers rock, rock (fist) breaks scissors, and scissors (move first two fingers like a scissors) cut paper. All players put their fists out together to the beat of Rochambeau (Ro-Sham-Bo). On "Bo," each player forms either rock, paper, or scissors. Then everybody has to follow the rules.

Travel Games

A—My Name Is . . .

Here's a "fill in the blank" game that works its way through the alphabet. It's best when the pressure of keeping the rhythm going makes players work especially hard. Here's how a boy might start things off beginning with the letter A: "A—my name is Abner, my sister's name is Anne, we come from Alaska and we sell Axes." A girl might follow, "B—my name is Bertha, my brother's name is Bert, we come from Boston and we sell Beans. You get the idea—you're out when you can't complete the sentence or when you break the tempo.

Buzz

If you've got a head for numbers, buzz is for you. First, players pick a number from 2 through 9. That number becomes *buzz*. Once *buzz* is named, players take turns counting, starting with 1. If *buzz* is 3, whenever you get to a number that contains a 3 or is a multiple of 3, you must say *buzz*. Players who mess up are out, and counting starts over again from 1. The last player remaining wins. For a challenge, play bizz-buzz, picking two numbers instead of just one. One number is bizz, and the other is *buzz*.

Plate-O-Grams

This game has no winners or losers—just some funny messages. To start, somebody has to spot a license plate and read the letters on the plate to everyone. For example, the letters might be "B-R-G." Next, everyone thinks of a three-word message beginning with those letters. In this case, people might come up with "<u>B</u>ig <u>R</u>ound <u>G</u>lobs" or "<u>B</u>eware <u>R</u>abid <u>G</u>erbils." (You might want to allow "little" words so the plate-o-grams make more sense, for example, "My <u>B</u>rother is <u>R</u>eally <u>G</u>ross.")

Categories

This game is good for many ages, since it can be made as easy or as difficult as you want. It all has to do with categories. One person thinks of a category—any category. It could be colors, capital cities, sports teams, or anything you can think of. Then players take turns naming items in the category. The game ends when someone repeats something already mentioned or when players can't think of any other items in the category.

Alphabet Derby

This is a race to the end of the alphabet. To play, you must find all the letters of the alphabet—in order. Letters may be found on road signs, billboards, bumper stickers, license plates, etc. You don't have to announce each letter you find, but if asked, you must tell what letter you are on. If challenged, you should be able to say where you saw your letters. The first one to Z wins. (To make things go more quickly, you may want to agree that Q is the only letter that can be found out of order.)

20 Questions

This old standby is simple, but fun. One player thinks of something (anything you can see, smell, hear, or touch) and tells the others if it is animal, vegetable, or mineral. The others take turns asking "yes-or-no" questions to try to figure out what it is. At any time a player may use a turn to guess what it is. It's best to ask a lot of questions before you start guessing, but remember, you only have twenty questions. Whoever guesses right wins. You can play this game using other categories, too, like famous people, places, or whatever—be creative!

Songs to drive

The Twelve Days of Our Trip
(to the tune of "The Twelve Days of Christmas")

On the first day of our trip this is what I saw—
the baby throw up in the car.

On the second day of our trip this is what I saw—
two pick-up trucks and the baby throw up in the car.

Third day:	three dead skunks
Fourth day:	four minivans
Fifth day:	five backseat fights
Sixth day:	six broken headlights
Seventh day:	seven miles of road work
Eighth day:	eight cars a-speeding
Ninth day:	nine railroad crossings
Tenth day:	ten roadside rest stops
Eleventh day:	eleven cop cars hiding
Twelfth day:	twelve bumper stickers

Your Destination: 99 mi.

Backseat Border Blues
(to the tune of "This Land is Your Land")

This side is my side; that side is your side.
Let's get along now; this is a long ride.
You see this line here—please don't cross over.
One side for you and one for me.

I had my eyes closed—faked I was sleeping.
So you got greedy and started creeping.
Try that again, Bub, and you'll be weeping.
One side for you and one for me.

Just like I warned you—now you are crying.
And Dad is angry—now you are lying.
You had it coming, there's no denying.
One side for you and one for me.

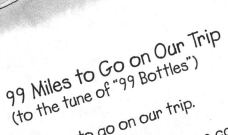

99 Miles to Go on Our Trip
(to the tune of "99 Bottles")

99 miles to go on our trip.
99 miles to go.
Step on the gas. I think we can pass.
98 miles to go on our trip. . .

(Keep repeating until you get to
"0 miles to go" or until someone
kicks you out of the car, whichever
comes first.)

the grown-ups CRAZY!

Are We Lost?
(to the tune of "Are You Sleeping?")

Are we lost? Are we lost?
Yes we are. Yes we are.
Someone get a map out. Someone get a map out.
Find the way. Find the way.

(Save this one for when you *really* get lost. Sing it as a round—as you drive around and around—and you're sure to drive the grown-ups crazy.)

Don't Get Out of the Fast Lane
(to the tune of "Take Me out to the Ball Game")

Don't get out of the fast lane.
Don't let up on the gas.
I can't believe all the cars we've passed—
Wherever we're going, we're going there fast.
And its zoom, zoom, zoom down the freeway,
But don't break the speed limit please.
Or the friend-ly Highway Patrol
Will request your keys!

Battle Hymn of the Brat
(to the tune of "Battle Hymn of the Republic")

Our minivan is loaded to the roof with games and toys.
We've all had snacks and found a station everyone enjoys.
The kids are all behaving well; we've hardly made a noise.
But something's not quite right.

(Chorus)
I'M NOT HAVING ANY FUN YET.
I'M NOT HAVING ANY FUN YET.
I'M NOT HAVING ANY FUN YET.
THIS TRIP IS DRAGGING ON.

We've hit every tourist trap from Maine to Monterey,
Miami to Mount Rushmore, Plymouth Rock to Frisco Bay.
We wait in never-ending lines forever and a day.
It's time to take a rest.

(Chorus)

Now you might think that I'm spoiled, that my attitude is bad.
You wouldn't be the first if my complaining makes you mad.
In fact you'd be the third, behind my Mother and my Dad.
But I still feel like this:

(Chorus)

When-You-Get-There

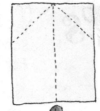
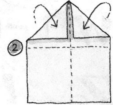
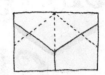
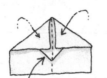
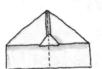

Paper Airplane Games

Find some paper and follow the paper airplane instructions. Then you can play games with your paper planes. 1) Go for distance. Whose plane can fly the farthest? 2) Fly for accuracy. Who can land closest to a chosen target? 3) Stay aloft. Whose plane can stay in the air the longest?

Fold, then unfold on ①④

Fold down corners. Fold down on line ②

Fold down corners again

Fold little flap up

Fold this side back to meet other side

Fold wings down on both sides

Hide the Doohickey

Any small object will do in this game that is fun for kids of all ages. One player hides the object while the others wait in another room. Players are then called back to find the object. Younger players might need to be told if they are "warm" or "cold." The first player to find the object gets to hide it next.

Bright Ideas

If you have a flashlight, you will never be bored again, at least not until you wear the battery out. Set up a flashlight in a dark room and make hand shadow figures on the wall. Tell a scary story while projecting a spider or a ghost onto the ceiling. Cut out shadow puppets and put on a show. With more than one flashlight you can play flashlight tag after dark—instead of tagging people, you hit them with your beam of light. A flashlight can also add a scary touch to face-making. Turn out the lights and see how scary you can look!

Learn to Girn

Face facts, faces are funny. Take your face to a mirror and see just how funny it can get. Serious face-makers call it "girning." It's even funnier if you have someone else to girn with. Work on blinks, winks, sneers, grimaces, grins, eyebrow raises, sidelong glances, or whatever. How many emotions can you show? How many faces can you make?

Games

Wastebasket H-O-R-S-E

A wastebasket makes a good indoor basketball hoop, and horse is a good indoor game. In horse, players take turns shooting for the hoop from various places on the court. Use rolled-up socks, crumpled-up paper or an appropriate indoor ball. If a player makes a shot, the next player must make it, too. One miss, and you get an H; two misses, an H-O; and so on. Miss five times and you are out with H-O-R-S-E.

Sock Soccer

This game is just like it sounds. Roll up some socks, set up some goals, agree on a rule or two, and start kicking. (WARNING: According to the American Sock Soccer Association, using lamps and plants for goalposts can get you in an awful lot of trouble!)

Slo-mo Volleyball

If you have any balloons left over from the water balloon toss, fill one with air for this slow motion, indoor version of volleyball. Play on your knees using a bed, couch, or some chairs for a net. You give up a point when you hit the balloon out, let it touch the ground, or fail to get it over in the agreed upon number of hits. Spike it, Dude, but don't let it pop!

Water Balloon Toss

In this damp contest, players pair up and form two lines facing each other. Each pair gets a balloon. One at a time, one person in each pair tosses the balloon to the other. After each successful toss, the tosser backs up a full step. The pair completing the longest toss wins and gets to stay dry! Most grown-ups will insist that you play this game outside.

Whirly-Bird

Make a simple paper helicopter using the instructions. Decorate your whirly-bird with markers or crayons before you cut it out. Drop your whirly-bird from a high place. When the wind is right, your whirly-bird will stay in the air for a long time. Watch it land, and then be sure to get it and fly it again.

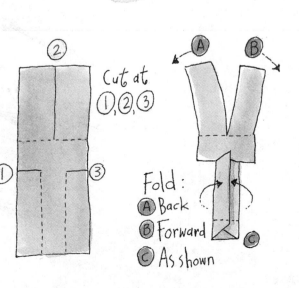

Cut at ①, ②, ③

Fold:
Ⓐ Back
Ⓑ Forward
Ⓒ As shown

Fold up

Knot Fun!

Grab some lanyard—you know, that brightly-colored plastic lacing. Then get busy making knots to create friendship bracelets, book marks, key chains, or anything else you can think of.

If you're making a bracelet, the quick knot and diamond knot work great because you start out with a loop. When you finish, tie the loose ends in an overhand knot that can slip through the loop to close the bracelet.

To make a key chain, start by attaching your lanyard to a key hook or ring. Then start knotting!

The Quick Knot

1. Cut one color of lanyard about 2 feet long. Cut another color about 3 feet long. Fold the shorter strand in half and tie it together with the longer strand, making sure you have a loop above the knot (see illustration). Hang the loop on something steady so you can use both hands to work.

2. Arrange the strands as shown in the illustration. The longer strand (A) will wrap around the shorter strands (B and C). First, cross strand A <u>over</u> strand B and <u>under</u> strand C. Then pull up on strand A so it's tight and close to the starter knot.

3. Next, cross strand A <u>over</u> strand C and <u>under</u> strand B. Then pull strand A tight again.

4. Keep going back and forth following steps 2 and 3 until you're finished.

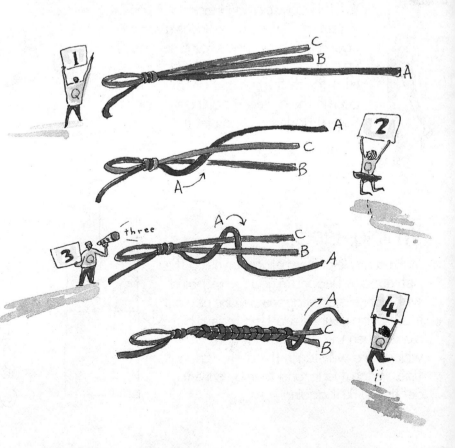

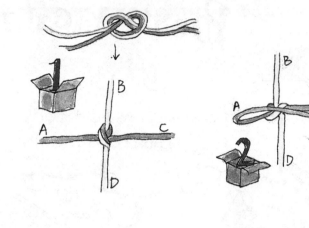

The Box Knot

1. Start with two colors of lanyard. Cut a piece from each color exactly the same length. You'll need a lot of lanyard for this knot, so figure on using strands that are at least 4-feet long, depending on what you're making. Put the two pieces together, making a regular overhand knot in the center. Spread out the strands so one color is in a line going up and down and the other color in a line going left and right. You now have four strands (A, B, C, and D).

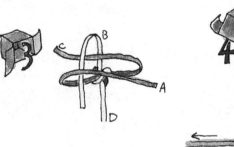

2. To begin the box knot, cross strand A right and strand C left leaving loops you can weave under and over as shown in the illustration.

3. Next, bring strand B down, crossing <u>over</u> strand C and <u>under</u> strand A.

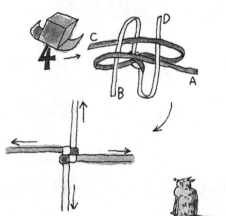

4. Then, bring strand D up, crossing <u>over</u> strand A and <u>under</u> strand C. Now pull on all the strands to tighten the knot. Continue following steps 2–4 to make more box knots.

The Diamond Knot

1. Grab two different colors of lanyard, each about 3 feet long. Fold each strand in half and tie the strands together at the top, making sure you have a loop above the knot (see illustration). Now you have four strands of equal length. Keep two strands of one color on the right and two strands of the other color on the left. Hang the loop on something steady so you can use both hands to work.

2. Cross strand D <u>under</u> strands C and B and <u>over</u> strand B as shown in the illustration.

3. Next, cross strand A <u>under</u> strands B and D and <u>over</u> strand D. (This is kind of tricky, but don't give up—keep practicing.) Then, pull up tightly so the diamond knot is close to the starter knot.

4. Start your next knot and keep following steps 2 and 3 until your creation is just the right length.

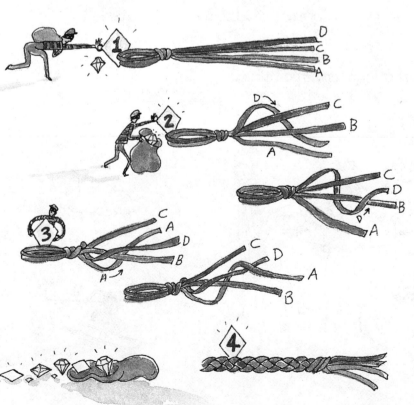

Best vacation ever!

Create your own crazy story. Ask somebody for words to fill in the blanks below.
Then read the story aloud.

_____ says that the best vacation ever is a _____ trip to _____.
PERSON'S NAME   NOUN   PLACE

Once you're there, you just have to _____. And don't forget to _____. The most exciting
                                        VERB   VERB

things to do are _____ and _____, but only if you're wearing _____.
                   ACTIVITY   ACTIVITY   TYPE OF CLOTHING

There's _____ food to eat, too. Order the _____ and _____ special
         ADJECTIVE (describing word)   NOUN   NOUN

for a real treat, and tell them _____ sent you. Before you head home, be sure to buy
                                  PERSON'S NAME

a _____ at the souvenir shop! It will always remind you of your _____ trip.
   NOUN   ADJECTIVE (describing word)